Original title:
A Fern in the Sun

Copyright © 2025 Creative Arts Management OÜ
All rights reserved.

Author: Jasper Montgomery
ISBN HARDBACK: 978-1-80581-900-4
ISBN PAPERBACK: 978-1-80581-427-6
ISBN EBOOK: 978-1-80581-900-4

Emerald Dreams Unfurled

In the garden, they dance and sway,
With whispers of green in a playful display.
Wearing sunlight like a silly crown,
They tickle the ground, never feel down.

In their company, laughter thrives,
They tease the gnomes, those static lives.
With cheeky curls, they shove and shove,
Chasing shadows like a playful love.

Fronded Reflections

These leafy jesters, bold and spry,
In a sunlit patch, they wave goodbye.
They hide from the rain, make clouds feel blue,
Pretending they're stars in the morning dew.

A potted friend on a window high,
Shooting glances to the sky with a sigh.
"Why climb mountains when you can just sway?
The breeze is an adventure, come what may!"

Radiating Life

With a wink and a nod, they dance on the floor,
Caught in the sun like never before.
Every droplet of water brings giggles galore,
They share inside jokes with the sweet garden floor.

The neighbor's cat looks on with disdain,
As they spin and twist without a care or pain.
"Let's party!" they murmur in leafy delight,
While the cat just glares; oh, what a sight!

A Canvas of Green Glow

Bright green splashes upon the ground,
Amongst the weeds, they dash around.
Their laughter echoes through the trees,
As they tickle the air with the softest breeze.

They dream of rainbows after the rain,
Crafting their stories, never mundane.
With each happy frond, they goofily boast,
In this canvas of laughter, they're the proud hosts.

Whispers of Green Beneath the Light

A leaf once tried to do a dance,
Twisting and turning, it took a chance.
But a breeze came by with a playful shove,
And whispered, "Buddy, you've no legs to shove!"

Sunlit giggles filled the air,
As critters laughed without a care.
"Flutter and hop, but stay down low,
Foliage prancing? You steal the show!"

Fronds Embracing Daybreak

Early morn, the fronds were found,
Jigging and jiving, making sound.
"We greet the sun with moves so slick,
Just watch us shine, it's quite the trick!"

But as they boogied, one got stuck,
Caught in a beam, oh what bad luck!
"Hey, grab my stem, I'm doing my best!
Just pull me down from my leafy nest!"

Sun-Kissed Shadows of a Leaf

In the garden, shadows play,
As leaves crack jokes throughout the day.
"Why did the stem refuse the sun?
Too hot today—this leaf won't run!"

A shadow snickered, then crossed the lane,
"Stand still, my friend, it's not in vain!
Let's take a rest, find cool ground to lie,
Where rays can't reach, we'll say goodbye!"

Luminous Greens in the Gloaming

At dusk, the greens began to chat,
"Have you seen that squirrel? He looks like a brat!"
They giggled and wiggled under fading light,
While shadows stretched long, what a silly sight!

"Let's throw a party, invite the bugs!
Bring twinkling fireflies and some warm hugs!
We'll dance till the night sings a lullaby,
Just hope the raccoon doesn't stop by!"

Light's Gentle Serenade

In the garden, a green chap fell,
Tickled by rays, oh what a swell!
Waving to bugs, and giving a wink,
He chuckled aloud, 'Come join me to stink!'

With a twist and a jig, he danced on the ground,
While nearby bees buzzed, all merry and sound.
The sun laughed back, shining through trees,
A comedy show with a light summer breeze!

Sway of the Sunned Leaves

Leaves caught in sunlight, a joyous parade,
Giggling softly, in shadows they played.
Bouncing and swaying, a leaf-gang so spry,
'Catch me if you can!' they called with a sigh.

The ants marched in rows, all tidy and neat,
But the leaves just laughed, 'You can't handle our beat!'
They jiggled and jostled, what a sight to behold,
Even the flowers sighed, 'We're left out in the cold!'

Fronds Awakened by Light

A sleepy green frond started to stretch,
Shaking off dreams that made him a wretch.
'Is that the sun's grin? Oh, what a delight!'
He twirled like a dancer, basking in light.

Greeting the morn with a flourish and flair,
He yawned and proclaimed, 'There's joy in the air!'
Bouncing and swirling, he felt so spry,
Till a squirrel passed by and made him cry 'Why?'!

A Dance in Dappled Rays

Dappled sunlight flickered, a playful tease,
Leaves began to giggle, swaying with ease.
Each shadow a chuckle, each ray a big grin,
A leafy ballet where all friends join in.

They twirled and they whirled, in frolicsome fun,
'Watch out for the critters!' they shouted in pun.
The show steals the day, a festival bright,
As nature performed under laughter and light!

Under the Solstice Shade

In the garden where I lay,
A leafy friend starts to sway.
Waving hello with a cheeky grin,
Dodging shadows like it's a win!

With each tick of the clock, it beams,
Crafting sunlight into dreams.
Dancing on breeze, a silly sight,
Glowing green, it's pure delight!

Nature's Symphony of Light

Beneath beams that sparkle bright,
Leaves are clapping with all might.
Beetles join in, quite the band,
Making music, oh so grand!

The sun's rays play hide and seek,
While whispers of wind seem to speak.
Bouncing laughter, nature's jest,
Life's a party; we're all blessed!

The Essence of Sun-Drenched Green

Oh how the green does laugh and shine,
With sun-kissed edges, just divine.
Its playful jig in morning's glow,
Reminds us all to let things flow!

Bug-eyed critters join the fun,
Cheering loudly as they run.
Bright hues flicker, what a scene,
Nature's heart is laughing keen!

From Shadows to Shimmer

In the corners, shadows creep,
But the vibrant green won't sleep.
It stretches tall, a comic act,
With every move, a little quacked!

Sunshine bursts like jokes well-timed,
While nature's laugh is well-chimed.
With every beam, a chuckle low,
In this green world, joy will grow!

Light Through a Frond's Embrace

In the garden, a dance takes flight,
Leaves flirt with rays, oh what a sight!
Nature's green, a cheeky tease,
Whispers secrets in the breeze.

Sunbeams tickle, laughter rings,
In the shade, the jester sings.
A playful twist on leafy charm,
Hilarity drapes, a leafy arm.

With each rustle, giggles grow,
Jokes sprout where the petals flow.
Poking fun at sky so blue,
A punchline made for me and you.

So raise a glass to green delight,
In this frolic, everything's bright.
For in the frond where sunlight reigns,
Life's a jest, with no more pains.

In the Warmth of Nature

Underneath the leafy dome,
Nature's warmth feels like home.
A tickle from the sunlit beams,
Sends the ferns into silly dreams.

With every breeze, a cheeky sway,
Green creatures giggle all the day.
They wave their fronds, a leafy cheer,
As if to say, 'Come join us here!'

Sunshine smiles with playful glee,
Whispers jokes from tree to tree.
Nature's humor, wild and free,
Laughing along with you and me.

So join the fun, don't miss a chance,
In this green-lit, froggy dance.
Let nature's giggle fill the air,
And leave behind your every care.

A Tapestry of Light and Leaf

In a patch of sunlit gold,
Leaves play games that never get old.
Draped in laughter, they defy,
Forget the clouds, just wave goodbye.

Here a giggle, there a grin,
Frolicking under the thickest skin.
Each frond spins tales of joy anew,
Crafting mischief in the dew.

Nature's canvas, bright and bold,
Humorous patterns start to unfold.
Beneath the sky, they weave and tease,
Turning silence into a breeze.

So let the laughter light the way,
In this greenery of a sunny day.
For as long as the leaves are green,
Life's a joke, let's hear it keen!

Ephemeral Green

A splash of green, a quick surprise,
Leaves wink beneath the bluest skies.
With every gust, they twist and twirl,
Nature's comic, a joyful whirl.

Shadows play in the jiggly sun,
Frogs croak back, 'Oh, that was fun!'
Life and laughter, quick and fast,
In moments fleeting, a spell is cast.

Underneath the vibrant tree,
Ferns chuckle quietly, oh-so free.
Jokes they weave in the sunny glow,
A fleeting moment, don't be slow.

So let's embrace this joyous scene,
Where every leaf holds life's routine.
In this patch of laughter, we convene,
To relish all things ephemeral green.

Spirals Upon the Soil

In the garden, green curls sway,
Dancing like they've found a play.
Wiggles and giggles in the breeze,
Whispers of joy from the leaves with ease.

Sunbeams tickle, leaves all grin,
No worries in the breeze, only fun to spin.
Roots chuckle underneath the dirt,
Fashioning jokes like they're experts in flirt.

Mischief sprouts at every turn,
Tickling toes that often burn.
Photosynthesis? More like photo-silly,
As plants laugh uncontrollably, oh what a frilly!

So if you wander, don't frown or pout,
Join in the laughter, let it sprout.
Nature's balloons in a dapper display,
Bringing sunshine to every green ballet.

Ferns in a Golden Hour

In the sun's glow, ferns wear crowns,
Swaying and dancing, no sign of frowns.
With each gentle wave, they take a bow,
Looking quite dapper, wouldn't you allow?

Golden light spills, a comic show,
Leaves flexing muscles, oh so slow.
Ticklish tendrils reach for a laugh,
Like they're in a quirky dance class half-bath.

Chirpy birds cackle in the trees,
Joining the fun with a light summer breeze.
Nature's own circus, quite a delight,
Ferns lead the way, dancing all night.

So take a peek in this green-gold hour,
Where laughter blooms like a vibrant flower.
In the garden's embrace, let your heart twirl,
For silly fern fun makes the whole world whirl.

Bright Whispers of the Forest

In the woods where shadows play,
Leaves giggle softly, leading the way.
Bright whispers echo, a cheeky tease,
Nature's rascals dance in the breeze.

With every rustle, the forest laughs,
Tickling the trunks and the chubby chaffs.
Branches high five, a jolly affair,
While critters prance without a care.

Mossy blankets catch a bright joke,
Spreading cheer like a playful cloak.
Together they chuckle, side by side,
In this green giggle, they take pride.

So visit the woods, let your spirits rise,
Join the bright whispers under the skies.
In nature's theater, let's all take part,
For funny foliage lifts every heart.

Illuminated Growth

When dawn breaks with a golden smile,
Plants stretch out, taking their while.
In each stretch, a tiny joke,
As shadows play beneath the oak.

Light filters down like candy rain,
Every leaf feasting, no sign of pain.
Giggly sproutlings wobble about,
Their lighthearted ballet, a whimsical shout.

With swaying roots and bouncing stems,
Nature's jesters don their gems.
In this theater of sun and shade,
Where every plant is lovingly made.

So let's join in this joyous show,
Where laughter with sunlight steals the glow.
In every twirl and joyful leap,
Nature's humor helps our spirits keep.

The Lush Embrace of Day

In the light, I tiptoe bright,
With leaves that dance, what a sight!
A giggle from the branches so spry,
As squirrels wave and birds all fly.

Beneath the shade, I find my spot,
Where sunbeams join in a playful plot.
The roots around me, cozy and snug,
Whisper secrets with a leafy hug.

A bumblebee buzzes with flair,
While ladybugs waltz through the air.
With each soft rustle, laughter grows,
Nature's humor is how it flows.

So lift your head, let joy be spread,
In this bright world, no room for dread.
For every shadow brings a jest,
A sunny life is truly best!

Sylvan Serenity

In the wood, a jig begins,
Where every critter wants to spin.
The pines chuckle and sway so high,
While clumsy raccoons pass by shy.

The brook sings jokes, splashes of cheer,
Filling the forest with glee, oh dear!
A deer trips up with a thump and a clout,
While rabbits roll, no worries about.

Leaves laugh soft in the gentle breeze,
As ants march on, they tease with ease.
"Catch us if you can!" they taunt and glide,
While lizards bask, full of pride.

So come take a stroll, it's pure delight,
Each shadow and beam is a playful sight.
Nature's comedy is on display,
In this leafy realm, come dance, come play!

Tranquil Brightness

Under a bright and sunny arc,
The garden plays, the joy is stark.
Mice with hats and snails in line,
Each moment feels like sipping wine.

The daisies giggle, swaying slow,
While butterflies put on a show.
With every bloom, a wink appears,
Nature's antics bring us cheers.

In the warmth, we sit and chat,
A wise old tortoise calls out, "Hey, bat!"
His shell is shiny, his tales are grand,
As we all laugh, hand in hand.

So let's bask in this golden light,
Where chuckles blossom, pure delight.
With every petal, a story spun,
In this bright world, we all have fun!

Hushed Communions

In twilight's glow, the whispers start,
A playful breeze, a cheeky dart.
The shadows dance, as if in jest,
We gather close, no time for rest.

The owls hoot softly, what a laugh,
As fireflies glow, our own photograph.
The stars above blink with a tease,
Inviting all to sit with ease.

Tiny fairies join the throng,
Beneath the trees where we belong.
Their giggles echo, a lively tune,
As we sway to the laughter of the moon.

With every hush, the fun expands,
In this secret world, where no one stands.
So lean in close, hear nature's song,
In these hushed moments, we all belong!

Serene Sunlit Existence

In a patch of light I lay,
My leafy friends dance and play.
One claimed a sunbeam as a throne,
Said he'd never be alone.

A bug flies by with a buzzing tune,
I wave goodbye, he's gone too soon.
With laughter shared and shadows cast,
I chuckle, this joy will forever last.

Underneath a Sky of Gold

With sunbeams wearing golden hats,
I spotted squirrels in acrobatic chats.
One slipped and tumbled with a squeak,
I couldn't help but laugh, so unique!

The clouds drift by, like cotton candy,
While birds sing songs, just a bit dandy.
In this world, oh so bright,
Even shadows bring delight!

Glowing Canopies

Leaves above like a jolly parade,
Whispering secrets, never afraid.
One said, "I've seen a flying shoe,"
I rolled with laughter; it can't be true!

The sun peeks through with a playful grin,
Casting spots where giggles begin.
In this playground of nature's design,
Even grumpy rocks can shine!

Forests of Warmth

In a tangled mess of green delight,
A rabbit popped up, what a sight!
He wore a hat, quite out of place,
Declared it was his running race!

I cheered him on as he hopped away,
Stumbling on twigs in a comical sway.
This forest, alive with silly cheer,
Wraps us all in its warmth, so near.

Awakening in the Sun

In the morning light, I shake and squirm,
Like a sleepy dog, I twist and turn.
With dew on my leaves, I bask with glee,
Whispering secrets to the buzzing bee.

I see the squirrels, they're quite a sight,
Dancing around, oh what a delight!
Their nimble feet tap a jig on the ground,
While I just giggle, in beauty I'm crowned.

Dappled Memories

Sun beams peek through a leafy crown,
Tickling my fronds, making me frown.
Do they dance like me in this sunny spree?
Nature's a clown, and I'm its marquee.

A butterfly floats, doing tango in flight,
Making me laugh with its vibrant delight.
It trips on a twig and lands with a plop,
While I cheer it on, I just can't stop!

The Alchemy of Green

Turning sunlight into laughter, it seems,
Each ray a potion, mixing dreams.
I wiggle and wiggle, a leafy ballet,
While the clouds giggle in their fluffy ballet.

The breeze sneezes, oh what a sound!
I shake and I shiver, spinning around.
What a ruckus in this vibrant fun,
Life is a jig under this glowing sun!

Ferns and the Day's Glow

With sun-kissed edges, so bright and bold,
I tell silly tales that never get old.
My neighbors, the daisies, roll on the floor,
Laughing and spinning, they beg for more.

The sun tickles toes in a warm, soft tease,
While I do the cha-cha with elegant ease.
Oh, what a life, in this dappled show,
Beneath the vast sky where laughter can grow.

Daylight's Embrace in the Verdant Wild

In the morning, leaves do dance,
Chasing sunbeams, taking their chance.
With each rustle, they start to tease,
Tickling the air like a playful breeze.

Wiggly worms, in a line, do crawl,
While squirrels giggle, so proud and small.
A sunlit stage where shadows play,
Nature's own, come what may.

Frogs croak jokes in their slick, green suits,
Telling tales of sunshine and roots.
Every petal seems to get a joke,
While the dandelions giggle and poke.

With a wink from the cloud's fluffy face,
The garden turns into a lively place.
Laughter rings from every nook,
In nature's storybook, take a look!

Glowing Notes of Nature's Orchestra

In the woods, a raucous show,
A symphony of laughs, oh don't you know?
The crickets chirp their funny tunes,
While squirrels hoard their acorns like loons.

Birds in concert, with winged finesse,
Squawk like they've won the great dress mess.
Nature's jesters, the flowers beam,
Bouncing light like a funky dream.

The breeze, it snickers, in playful hues,
As it tickles blades, they giggle too.
Nature's pranks float on the air,
Each twist and turn a prankster's flair.

Amidst the green, life's laughter swells,
Echoes of joy in foliage dwells.
A meadow full of jolly sights,
Lit by the sun, with funny lights!

As Light Filters Through the Canopy

Sunbeams peek, like little spies,
Through leafy curtains, oh what a surprise.
Whispers of joy, from branches high,
Tickling the ground with a playful sigh.

Underneath, critters gather round,
Chasing shadows across the ground.
The gentle rustle, a comical plot,
As leaves exchange gags without a thought.

Dancing dandelions share their tales,
Of windy trips and bumpy gales.
They shake their heads with a gentle tease,
Braving their antics like a light breeze.

In the shade, the world's a stage,
Where laughter blooms from every page.
Nature's jesters, in light's embrace,
Bring smiles and joy to every space!

A Tapestry of Fronds and Rays

In a patch of green, shades weave and twine,
Fronds frolic, declare, "This sun is mine!"
Laughing lightly with each swell and bend,
Nature's bouquet of a comic blend.

Bouncing bumblebees hum their songs,
Joining the chorus of nature's throngs.
With petals like hats and stems in a twist,
They join the fun; none can resist.

Giggling grasshoppers leap with cheer,
Spreading joy with each jump, loud and clear.
In this green circus, the sun's so bright,
Creating mischief from morning to night.

Laughter blooms beneath the bright blue,
Every rustle whispers, "We love you!"
In this riot of colors, life on parade,
The sun smiles down on the jokes we've made!

Sunlit Secrets of the Forest Floor

In the shade where shadows play,
A secret dance to brighten the day.
Leaves whisper jokes with the breeze,
Sneaky sunlight, if you please!

Mushrooms giggle, sprouting tall,
Waving to critters, having a ball.
Squirrels laugh as they chase their tails,
While ants share stories of heroic trails.

A wily fox peeks from a hole,
Jokes about acorns, a cheeky soul.
The forest floor, a laugh-filled floor,
Where every creature wants to explore.

So when you wander, don't be shy,
Join in the laughter, give it a try.
For in this place, oh what a score,
Sunlit secrets, forever to adore!

Glimmers on Treetop Veils

Up high where the laughter soars,
A canopy hides all of nature's scores.
Glimmers dance on the leaves so bright,
As whispers turn day into night.

Parrots squawk with a comedic flair,
Telling tales of the lazy bear.
Swaying branches in silly jest,
Who's the tallest? They're all the best!

A raccoon slips, takes a dive,
Plopping down with a giggle alive.
Glimmers of joy, twinkling around,
Nature's stand-up, notably profound.

So peer up high, let your heart twirl,
Join in the laughter of this leafy world.
For when treetops smile, watch them unveil,
The glittering giggles on their veils!

Nature's Lace in Golden Beams

In sunlight's grasp, the lace unfurls,
Weaving tales in tiny swirls.
Each frond a joke, each stem a pun,
Nature's craft, oh what fun!

Golden beams tickle the ground,
While shadows tease without a sound.
Ladybugs prance in their shiny suits,
While grasshoppers bouncing, playing loops.

Dewdrops glisten like laughter's tears,
Capturing moments, calming fears.
In this quilt made of green delight,
Life's silly whispers take flight!

So embrace the humor, let it race,
In nature's lace, find your place.
With every beam that colors your day,
Join the joyous laughter at play!

A Symphony of Light and Green

A concert plays in the leafy scene,
With crickets strumming, so serene.
A symphony of chirps, a giggling band,
Where sunlight winks, so carefully planned.

Winds whistle tunes through the trees tall,
Echoes of laughter, a cheerful call.
Each blade of grass joins in the fun,
Together they sway, under the sun.

Fireflies blink in the twilight haze,
Casting chuckles in dimming rays.
Nature's jesters, in rhythm they prance,
Inviting you all to join the dance.

So listen closely, hear the glee,
In every note, wild jubilee.
For in this green stage, under vast sky,
A symphony of joy, come dance and fly!

Cairn of Ferns

In the garden, green hats dance,
Poking out from a sunlit trance.
Whispers of leaves, secrets in the breeze,
Holding court with the buzzing bees.

Tickled toes on a grassy floor,
They flip and flop, oh what a chore!
Waving hands, a posh parade,
Crowning their heads in leafy braid.

Each stalk winks from behind a rock,
Making shadows, like a clock.
Stop the time, the sun's a trick,
With green comedians, oh so quick!

In this laughing patch, we lay,
As ferny jesters steal the day.
Beneath the hue of verdant gleam,
Life's a joke—just giggle and dream.

Grove of Glimmering Memories

Beneath the trees where shadows fight,
Little ferns hold court in light.
Each play a memory in the shade,
A dance of leaves in masquerade.

They wiggle, cackle in the air,
Telling tales beyond compare.
Glimmers of laughter, glints of glee,
In the grove, it's party spree.

Two left ferns step on a toe,
Oops! That's not how this dance should go!
With tipsy fronds asserting grace,
A leaf-ball brawl—a leafy race.

All the leaves have stories to tell,
Of sunshine lost and rainy spells.
In this grove where joy persists,
Ferny memories can't be missed.

Sunlit Fragments of Life

Between the cracks of morning light,
Sprightly ferns take a bold flight.
With outstretched leaves, they do a jig,
Bouncing along—oh how they wig!

Like kids in puddles, splashing round,
They flip and twirl without a sound.
Chasing sunbeams, feeling spry,
Living just to laugh and sigh!

Each frond a story, each sway a tease,
Sipping on sunshine with the bees.
With petals grinning, they take a chance,
Inviting all to join their dance!

Fragments of joy in the daytime glow,
Sprinkled with laughter, watch them grow!
In this sunny patch, life's a cheer,
With ferns that giggle, never fear!

Epiphany of Green

In a patch of light, the green folks prance,
Holding court in their leafy dance.
Amidst the humor, a lesson here,
Life's richer with laughter sincere!

Hey, watch that sprout! It just tripped!
Rolling about, oh how it flipped!
Every tumble brings giggles forth,
In this garden, joy has worth.

Twirling fronds in a sunny glow,
Telling secrets that only they know.
The roots are strong, but the fun runs wild,
Nature's wisdom as a playful child.

So join the ruckus, embrace the clean,
Laughter grows in shades of green.
In sunny meadows where giggles gleam,
Life's a jest, a joyful dream!

Radiance Among Leaves

In the garden, a wacky sight,
Leaves wearing sunglasses, so bright.
They gossip and giggle, it's true,
Fashion show for the morning dew.

A beetle struts by, full of flair,
He claims he's the best dressed insect there.
The daisies blush, a bit overdone,
While the sun gives a smile, just for fun.

The wind starts to dance, twirling around,
Tickling the branches, not making a sound.
Laughter erupts from the roots below,
As shadows join in the leafy show.

So if you stroll where sunshine gleams,
Join in the antics, fulfill your dreams.
Among the leaves, let your troubles flee,
In the backyard gala, come dance with me!

Sunlit Veins

In the sunlight, a story unfolds,
Veins of green, each secret told.
They whisper to clouds, what's the fuss?
Laughter escapes, it's a vibrant plus.

The brazen ants march in a parade,
Their tiny feet dance, oh what a cascade!
They tease the shadows, play 'tag' with the rays,
Under the sun, they frolic for days.

A flower sneezes, pollen takes flight,
Waving goodbye to a snoring sprite.
With a chuckle, the petals sway,
Creating a hat for a bumblebee's play.

So when you wander, stop and stare,
At the comedy show of the bright daytime air.
Join in the fun, let your heart combust,
For life's too short not to frolic in trust!

The Dance of Chlorophyll

Chlorophyll dreams of the limelight,
Dancers in green, such a glorious sight.
With pirouettes on the sun-warmed ground,
They twirl and spin, without making a sound.

A squirrel nearby, with acrobatic flair,
Tries to join in, but gets stuck in mid-air.
The leaves laugh out loud, oh what a tease,
While the sun chuckles down, waving a breeze.

The daisies are clapping, quite out of tune,
Cheering for ferns under a laughing moon.
The branches applaud, it's quite the affair,
In the limelight of photosynthetic air!

So hush now, dear friend, let the show begin,
Nature's cabaret, let the laughter spin.
Celebrate life with a playful embrace,
In this verdant theatre, find your place!

Verdant Solitude

In a nook of green, where the wild things wave,
Plants sing to the sky, a brave heart to save.
With quirky roots tangled in comic relief,
They share silly tales with a fallen leaf.

A shy sprout peeks out, just to have fun,
Cracks jokes with the shadows, laughing at sun.
The breeze carries giggles, tickles the ground,
As the clouds over yonder roll in all around.

With every flutter, let joy reincarnate,
Ticklish moments from early to late.
In silence they flourish, each laugh a burst,
In this lush, green haven, where worries disperse.

So stroll through the greenery, embrace the delight,
A world filled with laughter, oh what a sight!
For solitude sparkles with humor and bliss,
In the garden of giggles, you won't want to miss!

Sunbeams on Untamed Growth

In the garden, plants dance around,
A sunflower twirls, without making a sound.
The leaves gossip, under bright rays,
Critiquing the daisies in their silly ways.

The beetles parade, with tiny top hats,
While butterflies join in, wearing their spats.
The grass chuckles as the breeze takes a trip,
Swaying its blades, in a nature's flip.

A squirrel sneezes, as it jumps from a bough,
While the daisies blush, pretending to bow.
The sunbeams giggle, painting the scene,
In a world where the grass is comically green.

The moon rolls its eyes, when daylight breaks free,
Shouting, "Hey sun, let's keep this a spree!"
The bright laughter echoes, through nature's dome,
As flowers and critters call this place home.

Nature's Luminous Embrace

A lighthearted breeze whispers, 'Let's play!',
Tickling the petals throughout the day.
The sun winks at shadows, making them dance,
Nature's own stage in a whimsical trance.

Butterflies chuckle, flashing their styles,
While the buzzing bees compete with their smiles.
Each leaf has a story, a secret to share,
On how they disguise in sun-kissed flair.

The trees play charades, their branches sway high,
Pretending to be parrots, they mimic the sky.
With laughter like raindrops, the flowers confide,
In this joyous embrace, with nature as guide.

Each sunbeam a whisper, full of delight,
Filling the world with a giggly light.
In this merry tableau, life revels and beams,
Where all trees and blossoms fulfill their dreams.

The Sunlit Canopy

Under the bright canopy, laughter takes flight,
Winking leaves say, 'Is this fun or a fright?'
Beneath the big branches, critters all grin,
As sunlight spills down, like a game we can win.

A humorous breeze nudges each tree trunk,
Changing the mood from serious to funk.
Mice swapping puns with a tall, stately oak,
While fireflies wink, telling their jokes woke.

The path is a runway for ants dressed in ants,
Marching with swagger, showing off their pants.
Every sunlight sprinkle, a beacon so wild,
Nature's own children playing free, like a child.

As day waves goodbye, and night pulls a sheet,
The sun drops a wink, a mischievous treat.
With giggles and shadows, the nightbirds take wing,
In the sunlit canopy, endless joy does cling.

Shadows Play on Ferns

Where shadows frolic, they play hide and seek,
With leafy companions, both bold and unique.
A fern fits right in, with its delicate fronds,
Making side comments about the towering blonds.

The sunlight flickers, a playful disguise,
As flowers giggle at the ants' funny tries.
Each wiggle and jiggle brings joy from above,
As friends in the garden express all their love.

With whispers of humor, the shadows engage,
In a long-standing rivalry, nature's own stage.
The ferns sway along, enjoying the show,
A quirky round dance in the sunlight's warm glow.

As dusk tiptoes in, with a twinkle of cheer,
The shadows retreat, but the fun won't disappear.
For tomorrow they promise to meet in their play,
Where the laughter of nature won't fade away.

Embracing the Warmth of the World

In a patch of light, a creature grins,
Wiggling its toes where the laughter begins.
With petals as fans, they dance in delight,
An audience of bugs, a comedic sight.

Under bright skies where the sunshine squad,
Gathers to celebrate the joy of the odd.
With giggles and wiggles, they play hide and seek,
While sunbeams tickle, making plants squeak.

Jolly and plump, the leaves sway and tease,
Daring the shadows to try and appease.
A chorus of chuckles in every green race,
Nature's own sitcom with sunlight for grace.

As night draws near, and the giggles fade,
The forest still chuckles, its fun never stayed.
With whispers of joy among roots that connect,
A zany soirée, which none can reject.

Sunshine Kisses the Heart of the Woods

Sun-kissed leaves whisper jokes to the breeze,
While shadows play tricks, and everyone sees.
A squirrel in shades, doing the splits,
Flips over branches, as the sunlight fits.

A beaming sun warms the ground down below,
While flowers spin tales of the things they know.
They laugh at the clouds, trying hard to poke,
Saying, "You can't rain now, we've got laughs to evoke!"

Beetles in bowties, they dance on the floor,
While petals confetti from branches that soar.
The sun plays a prank with a shower of light,
Turns the whole forest into a comic sight.

As daylight tiptoes to bid its farewell,
The woods share their secrets, they chuckle and yell.
A warm-hearted forest, where humor takes root,
In sunshine's embrace, no worries to suit.

Melodies of Light and Leaf

In a dance of shadows, bright tunes arise,
Leaves clap their hands under brilliant skies.
A chorus of chirps sends laughter around,
The sun joins the song, where joy can be found.

Merrily buzzing, the insects will hum,
As sunshine prances, making all creatures drum.
A confetti of petals, they flutter and swirl,
In this wild, jolly, sun-drenched world.

With silly shadows that skip and prance,
Each glimmer of light seems to spark a dance.
Giggling grasses tickle and sway,
In this funny play, sunlight steals the day.

As evening draws close, with colors so bold,
The tales of the day turn to legends retold.
In the garden of laughter where everything beams,
A melody of joy drifts through our dreams.

Serenity in Sun-Drenched Stillness

In stillness, a lizard relaxes in style,
Sunlight's a blanket, inviting a smile.
With a wink to the sky and a nod to the lane,
It claims its sunspot, declaring no strain.

Nearby, a flower is cracking a jest,
Saying, "I bloom brightest, just look at this vest!"
Petals in patterns, a riot of glee,
A garden of laughter, as happy as can be.

While shadows sit quietly, plotting their fun,
The sun sneaks a peek, and shouts, "I'm not done!"
Their clever antics give everyone cheer,
As warmth wraps the world, spreading joy far and near.

With twilight now creeping, the day starts to close,
Yet laughter still lingers where sunshine bestows.
In moments so silly, serene, and divine,
The humor of nature makes every heart shine.

Glade of Serenity

In a glade where shadows play,
Lies a creature, bright and gay.
With fronds so green, it waves hello,
Like a dancer in soft flow.

It giggles when the sun is near,
Tickling leaves, full of cheer.
Whispers to the breeze up high,
'Catch my moves, oh, don't be shy!'

Sipping light like sweet lemonade,
In the sun, it's not afraid.
Bouncing in the warm embrace,
With a smile upon its face.

All the forest comes alive,
In this party, we all thrive.
Throwing shadows, doing spins,
Nature's fun, where laughter wins!

Nature's Emerald Choreography

Emerald dancers take the stage,
Bowing low, they're all the rage.
In soft rhythms, they entwine,
With every twist, it's so divine!

The sunbeams giggle, shining bright,
Encouraging this leafy sight.
Fluffy clouds, they drift and dip,
As nature leads this playful trip.

Each slight breeze is like a joke,
Laughter rustling, leaves provoke.
Join the show, don't miss a beat,
With every frond, they groove and greet.

In this patch, the fun runs wild,
Every branch, a playful child.
Let's applaud with all our might,
For nature's dance, pure delight!

The Story of Sun and Soil

Once upon a time in green,
Sun and soil shared a scene.
One got warm, the other cold,
Together, a tale of gold.

Sunbeam tickled roots below,
'Come on up, let's steal the show!'
The soil giggled, full of mirth,
'You bring the light, I'll bring the earth!'

They crafted a whimsy blend,
A leafy partner, nature's friend.
Swirling shadows, laughing bright,
Underneath, a hidden light.

So if you wander through the green,
Listen closely, hear the keen.
Sun and soil, a playful lore,
A joyful journey, evermore!

Veins of Radiant Life

In the quiet, green attire,
Veins of life are full of fire.
Pulsing with a silly beat,
They dance along, oh so sweet!

Little critters stop and stare,
'What a vibrant life affair!'
Laughter bubbles from the ground,
As leafy friends spin around.

Every leaf, a story spun,
Underneath the shining sun.
In this lively leafy show,
Friendship blossoms, watch it grow!

With every flicker, colors gleam,
In the forest's wildest dream.
Join the fun, be part of it,
In this green, hilarious skit!

The Sway of Green in Morning Glow

In the dawn's embrace, they stretch and sway,
Bowing to the sun, in a playful display.
Dancing to the song of a gentle breeze,
Winking at the squirrels as they tease.

With laughter in leaves and whispers of green,
They swing to the rhythm of a daydream scene.
Chasing the shadows, oh what a sight,
Turning the forest into sheer delight.

Frolicking in the light, they giggle with glee,
Throwing shade on the ants, how silly they be!
With a twist and a twirl, they shine like stars,
Nature's own jokers, without any bars.

So here's to the green in the sun's warm glow,
Their laughter's infectious, just watch it flow.
In a world full of gray, they're nature's own jest,
Making every morning feel truly blessed.

Nature's Paintbrush on the Forest Canvas

Each leaf holds a tale, spun in bright hues,
A tricky delight, making up jokes to amuse.
A giggle here whispers, a chuckle there too,
Nature's own laughter, breaking through blue.

With strokes of bright green, they paint with such cheer,
Bouncing in sunlight, oh dear, oh dear!
Ripping the silence, they burst into song,
Frolicking merrily, where they all belong.

Ticklish and vibrant, they shimmer and glint,
Hiding from rabbits, not a moment to stint.
Jokes only nature knows, shared in the breeze,
Every rustle is laughter, among the tall trees.

So gather around for the leafy parade,
With nature's laughs echoing, all worries will fade.
Under this patchwork of colors and fun,
A canvas of joy, kissed by the sun.

Whispers of Greenlight

In the hush of the woods, a giggle takes flight,
Little whispers of green scatter left and right.
Tales of the wiggly worms, quite the fool,
Chasing shadows and dreams, like they're at school.

Bubbles of laughter from leaves when they meet,
Sharing secrets of sunshine, oh what a treat!
Dancing with glee, each frond plays a part,
Spreading joy in the air, a true work of art.

"Hey, look at me!" says a sprout with a grin,
"Let's play hide and seek, I'm sure I will win!"
While twirling and whirling in daylight's embrace,
These whispers of green create a lively space.

So come join the fray where the fun doesn't end,
Nature's own comedy, around every bend.
A symphony of chuckles, a riot of hue,
In the whispers of greenlight, there's joy anew.

Fronds and Shadows

Fronds frolic and sway, with shadows to play,
Tickling the ground on this bright sunny day.
Each twist and each turn, a game of delight,
Flipping from green to a shade of pure light.

Coyote's giggle echoes, a tune of pure cheer,
While fronds trade their secrets, as if to persevere.
"Who's the funniest plant?" one whispers in jest,
"Let's find out right now, put humor to test!"

The shadows come bouncing, shining with glee,
Creating a spectacle, wild and free.
With imaginary hats and a jolly old tune,
They fashion a circus beneath the bright moon.

So dance with the fronds and laugh with the shade,
In this verdant domain, let your worries fade.
For here in this green world, where humor grows wide,
Each frond is a comedian, with laughter as pride.

Reflection in Flora's Heart

In the garden, green and bright,
A plant giggles, oh what a sight!
Winking leaves, with secrets untold,
Making whispers loud, yet bold.

Dancing shadows, a merry chase,
Sunshine tickling every face.
The roots plot jokes beneath the ground,
While petals sway to laughter's sound.

Every bug just wants to play,
And leaves join in, so hip hooray!
The breeze becomes a merry friend,
In this joy that seems to never end.

With colors bright and spirits high,
This thriving patch will never die.
For in the heart of every bloom,
Lies laughter's echo, filling the room.

Radiance on Silhouette

Light beams dance on leafy dreams,
Making shadows giggle at their schemes.
A playful breeze starts to hum,
While tiny critters tap their drum.

Every leaf a stage for fun,
In their world, the brightest sun.
A cactus joins, though feeling shy,
Pares away the prickles, oh my!

Laughter blooms in every bay,
As petals sway and twist away.
Even thorns join in the song,
Breaking silence, where they belong.

So stand and gaze, oh what a sight,
Where shadows dance in pure delight.
Nature winks with that glowing gleam,
In this garden, life's a dream.

A Saga of Leaves and Light

Once upon a time so green,
Lived a leaf with a quirky sheen.
It loved to prance under the sun,
Thinking life was just for fun!

With jokes about the roots below,
It entertained the plants in tow.
A wild flower joined the play,
Together they danced the day away.

Along came a snail, slow and spry,
Stumbled, slipped, but waved goodbye.
The humor spread from leaf to sun,
As giggles echoed—oh what fun!

In the end, when day was done,
The leaves agreed, we've truly won.
For laughter flows through every leaf,
In light they find their sweet belief.

Illuminated Fernery

In the shade where ferns take time,
To ponder jokes, and share a rhyme.
They chuckle at the spying sun,
And pass the time 'till day is done.

With roots that tangle in the fray,
They twist and turn in a comical way.
Each leaf a dancer on the floor,
Shaking it like never before.

A rabbit hops, and starts to play,
Inviting all to join the sway.
The ferns erupt with laughter bright,
As they bask in the warm moonlight.

So come along, let worries cease,
In the ferns, you'll find your peace.
For humor grows where hearts align,
In this leafy world, all's divine.

The Dance of Leaves in Daylight

In daylight's glow, they jig and sway,
The leaves in green, they laugh and play.
A twirl, a spin, a leafy jig,
They beckon bugs to join the gig.

With every breeze, they flap and flop,
From high above, they won't stop.
A conga line of nature's crew,
With joy they dance, all shiny and new.

Little critters join the fun parade,
A slip-up here, a wobbly fade.
A butterfly slips, a ladybug falls,
Laughter rings through leafy halls.

As daylight dims, the dance subsides,
While faeries giggle and the moonlight hides.
Yet leaves still chuckle in twilight's rest,
Ready to bounce, forever blessed.

Solstice Serenade in the Underbrush

In shadows deep, a song takes flight,
The underbrush hums, a funny sight.
Squirrels strum on twiggy strings,
The frogs join in, oh what joy it brings!

A hedgehog taps on a tiny drum,
While crickets chirp, they come undone.
A dance-off starts, who will win?
The beetle rolls, with a cheeky grin.

As sunlight beams, the crowd grows wild,
The woodland's ruckus, nature's child.
With every note, more shades appear,
Even the moss seems to cheer!

Soon twilight whispers, the show's at end,
But tomorrow's fun will just extend.
The underbrush laughs, a merry bunch,
Awaiting dawn, for another crunch.

Shadows Play in the Warmth

In sunlit corners, shadows prance,
They twist and turn, a playful dance.
A squirrel peeks, then disappears,
While sunbeams tickle all our fears.

In gaps and grooves, a game unfolds,
The light and dark, stories told.
A worm slides by, it winks and nods,
While beetles laugh and give their applauds.

With every step, a shadow grows,
In nature's charm, hilarity flows.
A stick gets stuck in a sunbeam's grip,
And through the air, a leaf takes a dip.

As dusk arrives, the games will cease,
Yet in our hearts, they hold their lease.
Tomorrow bring, more fun and play,
For shadows dance in a sunny way.

Verdant Reflections in a Sunlit Glade

In the glade where sunbeams luge,
Green reflections shout, 'Let's all cruise!'
The ferns wear shades, they feel so cool,
While daisies giggle, breaking the rule.

A caterpillar starts a trend,
In leafy outfits, they twist and bend.
While bees buzz by with style and flair,
A croaky toad declares, "Who cares?"

The sun dips low, a golden glow,
The glade throws a party, don't you know?
Each sprout and shoot prepares to cheer,
With froggy dances that draw near.

As nightfall wraps this verdant friend,
The laughter lingers, will never end.
Tomorrow brings another song,
In the sunlit glade, where all belong.

Radiance Upon the Fronds

In a forest of laughter, the green tales spun,
Fronds waving hello, basking in fun.
They giggle in shadows, a dance on the breeze,
While sunbeams tickle, they sway with ease.

A squirrel in shades, wearing shades of bright hue,
Sips on its acorn latte, oh-so-true.
The sun's golden rays, a hilarious sight,
As every green leaf shares jokes in daylight.

Fungi peek in, with a smirk they can't hide,
They laugh at the fronds when the sun's on their side.
A chorus of chirps joins the radiant fun,
In this merry green realm, where everyone's won.

So let's prance and twirl in this leafy parade,
Where the sunlight brings giggles, and shadows never fade.
With a wink and a nod, the day's taking flight,
Underneath all the fronds, everything feels just right.

Gentle Light on Verdant Dreams

Beneath the soft glow, where giggles take flight,
Whispers of the green share secrets tonight.
A dragonfly dances, with moves legendarily cool,
While the sun paints a picture, a radiant jewel.

The daffodils chortle, their heads held so high,
Claiming the throne as clouds float by.
Each rustle and shake sends a chuckle around,
In this verdant kingdom, silliness found.

Grass blades in uniforms stand at attention,
While ants march along with perfect intention.
But the sunlight's warm hug ensures all will play,
In this gala of greens, let's throw doubts away.

So gather the laughter beneath that bright beam,
In the gentle light, we'll chase every dream.
With shadows as partners and sunshine as guide,
Let joy be our anthem, let good vibes collide.

Dappled Hues in a Summer Grove

In a grove full of giggles, the colors collide,
Sunlight bursts in, leaving shadows to hide.
Each petal a joker, with stories to share,
While the breeze giggles softly, without any care.

A curious snail dons a cap far too tall,
Slowing the pace while enjoying it all.
The mushrooms chime in, their caps a bright cheer,
In this patch of delight, they have nothing to fear.

With a wink and a nod, the trees start to sway,
As laughter erupts in this fanciful display.
The daisies are snickering, gossiping away,
About the ways the sunlight makes mischief and play.

So let us embrace the humor that glows,
In dappled hues where the laughter freely flows.
Side by side with the whimsy, we'll dance and will sing,
In this summer grove, where the heart's always spring.

The Solstice of a Silent Leaf

A leaf in the sun, wearing a grin so bright,
Catches all the giggles as day turns to night.
With shadows now yakking, and rays in a tiff,
The world is a circus, and oh, what a whiff!

The breeze rolls in laughter, cheeky and spry,
Tickling the branches that wave up so high.
The clouds roll their eyes as they drift on by,
Making faces at sunbeams that can't help but sigh.

Every drop of each dew has a tale it must tell,
As laughter erupts in the magical swell.
The leaf winks at twilight, it knows all the jokes,
In this solstice of silliness, where laughter invokes.

So let's toast to the twilight, the giggles, the fun,
To leaves in the laughter, and moments begun.
With hearts leaping high, let's embrace all the cheer,
For in this whimsical world, there's no room for fear.

Swaying in Solar Breaths

In a garden quite absurd,
A leaf danced with a little bird,
They swayed in a rhythmic twist,
Nature's own frolicking mist.

The sun chuckled from above,
Watching antics with great love,
While shadows giggled on the ground,
In this joyous world, magic found.

Worms played tag without a care,
While daisies twirled in the air,
The sun drew smiles from each petal,
Every moment was light as a kettle.

So, if you peek and see them prance,
Join in their quirky, merry dance,
For life outside is simply fun,
In the light where laughter's spun.

Beneath the Gilded Sky

Beneath a sky that wore a grin,
A madcap bug jumped right in,
Splitting beams with socky style,
While daisies winked and flashed a smile.

The clouds puffed up like cotton candy,
While squirrels tried to act so dandy,
A breeze rolled through and tickled trees,
This sunny stage brought all to knees.

Each petal held a secret joke,
While crickets played their merry folk,
In shadows long, the laughter brewed,
And plants all sported leafy masks, imbued.

So if you sit and watch the fun,
Remember, laughter weighs a ton,
In gold-touched moments, let it flow,
Under the sky where chuckles grow.

The Secret Life of Leaves

While you're busy, sipping tea,
Leaves are whispering, 'Can't you see?'
They dive in puddles, splash around,
Making mischief without a sound.

Hidden in foliage, giggles burst,
Rolling down hills, it's the leaf's first,
They've got no thoughts of quiet days,
Only pranks and silly ways.

As the wind teases them to glide,
They play hide and seek, full of pride,
A twist and turn, a flutter free,
Life on high is pure jubilee.

For those who wander through this cheer,
Take a moment, lend an ear,
You might just hear their joyous call,
The secret life of leaves, after all.

Cradled by Luminescence

In twilight where shadows laugh and play,
A flower sought moonbeams to sway,
Cradled in glow, it danced so fine,
Underneath stars that sparkled in line.

With each breeze, it told a tale,
Of silly bugs and a leaf on a mail,
High up on branches, dreams took flight,
While crickets crooned into the night.

The moon stretched wide in stunning beams,
Casting light on all the plants' schemes,
They held a party, wild and bright,
Showing off their mischief, a fun delight.

So when the sun sets low and dim,
Remember, nature can be quite a whim,
For in the dark, the laughter finds,
Cradled by luminescence's binds.

The Tender Touch of Day's Embrace

In the morning glow, I sway and dance,
With whispers of light, I take a chance.
My leaves stretch wide, looking quite absurd,
As shadows laugh and chirps are heard.

A sunbeam tickles, a breeze does tease,
While ants prance by, with utmost ease.
'Look at me!' I shout, 'A sun-kissed show!'
The bugs just chuckle, 'You're putting on a glow!'

Basking in the Warmth of Midday

Under the bright and gleeful rays,
I frolic alone in a leafy haze.
Squirrels pause, with their nutty grin,
They point and jeer, 'What a awkward win!'

A butterfly twirls, on a dare so bold,
While I stand firm, despite feeling cold.
'You think I'm silly?' I jest in reply,
'Wait till you sprout a puffy tie!'

Sunlit Chronicles of a Woodland

Amidst the trees, in a sunny patch,
I overhear the critters hatch.
'Oh look at that leaf!' the rabbit squeaks,
'I'd wear it as a hat for weeks!'

The forest chuckles, a chorus bright,
As mushrooms brag about last night's fright.
'Is being green not a fashion trend?'
'The sun's no friend, it must end!'

The Awakening of Tender Leaves

As dawn unrolls in a playful cheer,
My tender tips sprout, without any fear.
I tease the dew, I dance on the ground,
While the daisies giggle, all around.

'Come play with us!' they beckon in jest,
'We'll twirl like wildflowers, we're the best!'
I take a bow, feeling quite spry,
Until a raindrop lands, oh my, oh my!

www.ingramcontent.com/pod-product-compliance
Lightning Source LLC
Chambersburg PA
CBHW070316120526
44590CB00017B/2700